INDULGENCE

cupcakes

39 irresistible sweet treat recipes

THUNDER BAY
P·R·E·S·S

San Diego, California

Contents

If you are using silicone molds in place of muffin tins and paper cases,
for the best result, grease the insides of the molds very lightly with vegetable oil
or butter so that the cooked cupcakes are easily turned out. For ease of handling,
place the filled molds on a baking tray before they go into the oven.

Family favorites

From naughty to nice, this delicious assortment
will bring out the child in all of us.

Orange poppy seed cupcakes

MAKES 15

¼ cup poppy seeds, plus extra to sprinkle
½ cup warm milk
½ cup plus 1 tablespoon unsalted butter, softened
3 teaspoons finely grated orange zest
¾ cup superfine sugar
2 eggs
1½ cups self-rising flour, sifted

Citrus frosting
1 cup unsalted butter, softened
3 cups confectioners' sugar, sifted
3 teaspoons finely grated orange zest

Preheat the oven to 350°F. Line 15 standard muffin cups with paper liners.

Combine the poppy seeds and milk in a bowl and set aside for at least 15 minutes.

Place the butter, orange zest, superfine sugar, eggs, and flour in a large bowl. Add the poppy seed mixture and beat with electric beaters on low speed until combined. Increase to a medium speed and beat for 3 minutes, or until the mixture is thick and pale.

Divide the mixture evenly among the paper liners. Bake for 15 minutes, or until a toothpick comes out clean when inserted into the center of a cake. Transfer onto a wire rack to cool.

To make the citrus frosting, place the butter, confectioners' sugar, and zest in a large bowl and beat with electric beaters until light and fluffy. Spread the frosting over the cakes and sprinkle with the extra poppy seeds.

Plum crumble mini cakes

MAKES 24

Preheat the oven to 350°F. Line 24 flat-based mini muffin cups with paper liners.

Cream the butter, sugar, and vanilla with electric beaters until light and creamy. Add the eggs one at a time, beating well after each addition. Sift the flours together and fold in alternately with the plum juice. Divide the mixture evenly among the paper liners and cover each with slices of plum.

To make the crumble topping, place the sugar, flour, and butter in a bowl. Mix together with your fingertips until it resembles coarse breadcrumbs. Sprinkle the crumble over each cake, covering the plums.

Bake for 15–18 minutes, or until golden. Transfer onto a wire rack to cool.

¾ cup unsalted butter, softened
¾ cup superfine sugar
1 teaspoon natural vanilla extract
3 eggs
1 cup self-rising flour
¼ cup all-purpose flour
½ cup canned natural plum juice
9 canned plums in natural juice, pits removed, thinly sliced

Crumble topping
½ cup raw sugar
1 cup all-purpose flour
heaping ⅓ cup unsalted butter, chilled and diced

9

Gingerbread cupcakes

MAKES 16

2 cups self-rising flour
¾ cup all-purpose flour
½ teaspoon baking soda
3 teaspoons ground ginger
1 teaspoon ground cinnamon
1 teaspoon pumpkin pie spice
1 cup soft brown sugar
¼ cup candied ginger, chopped
⅔ cup maple syrup
heaping ⅓ cup unsalted butter, chopped
1 cup buttermilk
2 eggs, lightly beaten

Ginger frosting
2 cups confectioners' sugar, sifted
1 teaspoon ground ginger
1 tablespoon unsalted butter, softened

Preheat the oven to 400°F. Line 16 standard muffin cups with paper liners.

Sift the flours, baking soda, ground ginger, cinnamon, and pumpkin pie spice into a large bowl. Stir in the brown sugar and candied ginger. Make a well in the center.

Put the maple syrup and butter in a small saucepan and stir over medium heat until melted. Remove from the heat and cool. Combine the syrup mixture, the buttermilk, and egg in a bowl, mix together and pour into the well in the dry ingredients. Fold in gently until just combined—the batter should be lumpy.

Divide the mixture evenly among the paper liners. Bake for 20–25 minutes, or until a toothpick comes out clean when inserted into the center of a cake. Transfer onto a wire rack to cool.

To make the ginger frosting, place the confectioners' sugar, ginger, and butter in a small heatproof bowl. Stir in enough warm water to form a smooth paste. Set the bowl over a saucepan of simmering water, making sure the bowl doesn't touch the water, and stir until smooth and glossy. Remove from the heat. Spread 2 teaspoons of frosting over each cake. Sprinkle with confectioners' sugar.

Hot cross bun cakes

2 cups self-rising flour
3 teaspoons ground cinnamon
½ cup unsalted butter, chopped
1 cup golden raisins
¼ cup mixed candied citrus peel
¾ cup superfine sugar
¾ cup milk
2 eggs, lightly beaten

2 teaspoons powdered gelatin
2 tablespoons superfine sugar

Frosting
½ cup confectioners' sugar
2 teaspoons lemon juice

Preheat the oven to 400°F. Grease 12 standard muffin cups.

Sift the flour and cinnamon into a large bowl, add the butter, then rub together with your fingertips until the mixture resembles fine breadcrumbs. Stir in the golden raisins, citrus peel, and superfine sugar. Make a well in the center.

Whisk the milk and egg in a bowl, then pour into the well. Fold in gently until just combined—the batter should be lumpy.

Divide the mixture evenly among the muffin cups. Bake for 20–25 minutes, or until the cakes come away from the side of the tin. Cool briefly, then transfer onto a wire rack.

To make the glaze, combine the gelatin, superfine sugar, and 2 tablespoons of water in a small saucepan. Stir over low heat for 1 minute, or until the sugar and gelatin are dissolved. Remove from the heat. Brush the glaze over the warm cakes a couple of times, then allow them to cool.

To make the frosting, mix the confectioners' sugar and lemon juice together until smooth. Spoon the frosting into a piping bag, and pipe a cross on each cake and allow them to set.

Jaffa cupcakes

MAKES 12

1⅓ cups self-rising flour
¼ cup unsweetened cocoa powder
1 cup superfine sugar
2 eggs, lightly beaten
⅔ cup milk
½ cup unsalted butter, melted
1 tablespoon finely grated orange zest

Orange buttercream
2 cups confectioners' sugar, sifted
¼ cup unsalted butter, softened
2 teaspoons finely grated orange zest
2 tablespoons orange juice
orange nonpareils, to decorate

Preheat the oven to 350°F. Line 12 standard muffin cups with paper liners.

Sift the flour and cocoa into a large bowl, then stir in the sugar. Add the egg, milk, melted butter, and orange zest and beat with electric beaters for 2 minutes, or until well combined and smooth.

Divide the mixture evenly among the paper liners. Bake for 18–20 minutes, or until a toothpick comes out clean when inserted into the center of a cake. Transfer onto a wire rack to cool.

To make the orange buttercream, place 1 cup of the confectioners' sugar, the butter, zest, and orange juice in a large mixing bowl. Beat with electric beaters until smooth and creamy. Gradually add the remaining confectioners' sugar and beat until the cream is thick.

Decorate each cake with buttercream and nonpareils.

Apricot, sour cream, and coconut cupcakes

MAKES 20

1¾ cups self-rising flour
½ cup unsweetened dried coconut
½ cup unsalted butter
1 cup superfine sugar
2 eggs, lightly beaten
1 cup apricot juice
½ cup sour cream
20 canned apricot halves in juice, drained
¼ cup apricot jam

Preheat the oven to 350°F. Line 20 standard muffin cups with paper liners.

Sift the flour into a large mixing bowl, then add the coconut and make a well in the center. Melt the butter and sugar in a small saucepan over low heat, stirring until the sugar has dissolved. Remove from the heat. Whisk the combined egg and apricot juice into the sour cream. Add both the butter and the egg mixtures to the well in the dry ingredients and stir with a wooden spoon until combined.

Divide the mixture evenly among the paper liners and place an apricot half, cut side up, on the top of each cake. Bake for 18–20 minutes, or until a toothpick comes out clean when inserted into the center of a cake. Transfer onto a wire rack to cool.

Heat the jam in a small saucepan until melted. Brush a little jam over each cake.

17

Butterfly cupcakes

MAKES 12

½ cup unsalted butter, softened
⅔ cup superfine sugar
1½ cups self-rising flour
½ cup milk
2 eggs
½ cup heavy cream
¼ cup strawberry jam
confectioners' sugar, to sprinkle

Preheat the oven to 350°F. Line 12 standard muffin cups with paper liners.

Beat the butter, sugar, flour, milk, and eggs with electric beaters on low speed until combined. Increase to medium speed and beat until the mixture is smooth and pale.

Divide the mixture evenly among the paper liners and bake for 15–20 minutes, or until a toothpick comes out clean when inserted into the center of a cake. Transfer onto a wire rack to cool.

Cut a shallow round from the center of each cake using the point of a sharp knife, then cut the round in half. Spoon 2 teaspoons of cream into the cavity of each cake, then top with 1 teaspoon of jam. Position the two halves of the cake round in the jam to resemble butterfly wings. Sprinkle with sifted confectioners' sugar.

Peanut butter mini cupcakes

MAKES 18

Preheat the oven to 350°F. Line 18 flat-based mini muffin cups with paper liners.

Beat the butter and sugar together in a bowl with electric beaters until light and creamy. Add the eggs, one at a time, beating well after each addition. Add the peanut butter and beat until combined. Fold in the sifted flours alternately with the milk until combined.

Divide the mixture evenly among the paper liners. Bake for 10–12 minutes, or until a toothpick comes out clean when inserted into the center of a cake. Transfer onto a wire rack to cool completely.

To make the hazelnut and peanut butter frosting, combine the hazelnut spread and peanut butter. Spread the frosting over each cake and decorate with a piece of candy bar.

scant ⅔ cup unsalted butter, chopped
½ cup soft brown sugar
2 eggs
½ cup crunchy peanut butter
1 cup self-rising flour
¼ cup all-purpose flour
¼ cup milk

Hazelnut and peanut butter frosting
½ cup hazelnut spread, softened
⅓ cup crunchy peanut butter, softened
2 x 2¼-ounce chocolate-coated candy bars, chopped

21

Jam doughnut cupcakes

MAKES 18

1¼ cups self-rising flour
½ cup superfine sugar
½ cup milk
2 eggs
1 teaspoon natural vanilla extract
½ teaspoon dried yeast
½ cup strawberry jam
1 tablespoon unsalted butter, melted
2 tablespoons cinnamon sugar

Preheat the oven to 350°F. Line 18 standard muffin cups with paper liners.

Combine the flour and sugar in a bowl, and make a well in the center. Put the milk, eggs, vanilla, and yeast in a bowl and whisk to combine. Pour into the well in dry ingredients and whisk until smooth.

Divide half the mixture evenly among the paper liners. Top each with 1 teaspoon of jam, then cover with the remaining mixture. Bake for 10–12 minutes, or until a toothpick comes out clean when inserted into the center of a cake. Brush a little melted butter over each cake, then dip it into the cinnamon sugar. Serve the cakes warm.

Honey, banana, and macadamia cupcakes

MAKES 32

Preheat the oven to 350°F. Line 32 mini muffin cups with paper liners.

Melt the butter and honey in a small saucepan, stirring until combined. Allow to cool.

Sift the flour and pumpkin pie spice into a large bowl. Add the carrot, banana, macadamias, eggs, and honey mixture, stirring until the mixture is just combined and smooth.

Divide the mixture evenly among the paper liners, and sprinkle the tops liberally with extra chopped macadamias. Bake for 8 minutes, or until a toothpick comes out clean when inserted into the center of a cake. Transfer onto a wire rack to cool.

Drizzle a little honey over the cakes before serving.

heaping ⅓ cup unsalted butter, chopped
1 cup honey, plus extra to drizzle
2 cups self-rising flour
1 teaspoon pumpkin pie spice
1½ cups coarsely grated carrot
1 ripe banana, mashed
½ cup chopped macadamia nuts, plus extra to sprinkle
2 eggs, lightly beaten

Half-moon cupcakes

MAKES 16

1 cup unsalted butter
1 cup superfine sugar
1 teaspoon natural vanilla extract
4 eggs
1½ cups self-rising flour, sifted
½ cup all-purpose flour, sifted
¾ cup milk
¼ cup unsweetened cocoa powder, sifted

Frosting
1½ cups confectioners' sugar, sifted
2 teaspoons unsalted butter

Chocolate topping
1⅓ cups chopped bittersweet chocolate

Preheat the oven to 350°F. Line 16 standard muffin cups with paper liners.

Beat the butter, sugar, and vanilla together with electric beaters until light and creamy. Add the eggs, one at a time, beating well after each addition. Fold in the flours alternately with the milk. Divide the mixture in half and stir the cocoa through one half of the mixture until well combined. Divide the chocolate mixture evenly into half of the paper liners. Then divide the plain mixture into the other half, so that each paper liner is filled with half chocolate and half plain mixtures. Bake for 18–20 minutes, or until a toothpick comes out clean when inserted into the center of a cake. Transfer onto a wire rack to cool.

To make the frosting, place the confectioners' sugar and butter in a small heatproof bowl. Stir in enough warm water to form a smooth paste. Set the bowl over a small saucepan of simmering water and stir until smooth and glossy. Remove from the heat. Spread the frosting over the white side of each cake.

To make the chocolate topping, place the chocolate in a small bowl over a saucepan of simmering water, and stir occasionally until the chocolate has melted. Spread the chocolate over the other half of the cakes.

Apple pecan cupcakes

MAKES 16

2½ cups self-rising flour
1½ teaspoons ground cinnamon
¾ cup superfine sugar
2 granny smith apples, peeled, cored
  and coarsely grated
½ cup pecans, chopped
2 eggs, lightly beaten
½ cup milk
3 teaspoons unsalted butter, melted
heavy cream or yogurt, to serve (optional)

Preheat the oven to 350°F. Line 16 standard muffin cups with paper liners.

Combine the flour, cinnamon, sugar, apple, and pecans in a bowl. Add the egg, milk, and melted butter, stirring until the mixture is just combined and smooth.

Divide the mixture evenly among the paper liners. Bake for 18–20 minutes, or until a toothpick comes out clean when inserted into the center of a cake. Transfer onto a wire rack to cool.

If desired, sprinkle with confectioners' sugar and serve with heavy cream or yogurt.

Beehive cupcakes

¾ cup plus 1 tablespoon unsalted butter, softened
1 cup soft brown sugar
3 eggs
⅓ cup honey, warmed
2¼ cups self-rising flour, sifted

Marshmallow frosting
3 egg whites
1½ cups sugar
2 teaspoons light corn syrup
pinch of cream of tartar
1 teaspoon natural vanilla extract
yellow food coloring
15 toothpicks
15 chocolate-foil wrapped bumble bees
with wings

Preheat the oven 350°F. Line 15 standard muffin cups with paper liners.

Beat the butter and sugar with electric beaters until light and creamy. Add the eggs, one at a time, beating well after each addition. Fold in the honey and flour until combined. Divide the mixture evenly among the paper liners. Bake for 18–20 minutes, or until a toothpick comes out clean when inserted into the center of a cake. Transfer onto a wire rack to cool.

To make the marshmallow frosting, combine the egg whites, sugar, corn syrup, cream of tartar, and 3½ fluid ounces of water in a heatproof bowl. Set the bowl over a saucepan of simmering water, making sure the bowl doesn't touch the water. Beat for 5 minutes with electric beaters, or until the mixture is light and fluffy. Remove from the heat. Add the vanilla and beat with electric beaters for 4–5 minutes, or until stiff peaks form. Add the coloring, drop by drop, and beat until just combined.

Spoon the frosting into a piping bag fitted with a ½-inch round nozzle, and pipe the frosting in circles around the cake to resemble a beehive. Push the pointy end of the toothpick into the base of each bee and insert it into each cake.

Mini pear and walnut cupcakes

MAKES 36

scant ⅔ cup unsalted butter, softened
¾ cup soft brown sugar
2 eggs
1¼ cups self-rising flour, sifted
½ cup milk
½ cup canned pears, well drained and chopped
⅓ cup chopped walnuts

Maple cream frosting
⅓ cup cream cheese, softened
¼ cup maple syrup
1½ cups confectioners' sugar, sifted
½ cup chopped walnuts, to decorate

Preheat the oven to 350°F. Line 36 mini muffin cups with paper liners.

Beat the butter and sugar together with electric beaters until light and creamy. Add the eggs, one at a time, beating well after each addition. Fold in the flour alternately with the milk. Fold in the pears and the walnuts. Divide the mixture evenly among the paper liners. Bake for 12–15 minutes, or until a toothpick comes out clean when inserted into the center of a cake. Transfer onto a wire rack to cool.

To make the maple cream frosting, beat the cream cheese and maple syrup with electric beaters until combined. Gradually beat in the confectioners' sugar until combined. Spread the frosting over each cake and decorate with chopped walnuts.

Milk chocolate buttons

Preheat the oven to 325°F. Line 12 mini muffin cups with paper liners.

Place the butter and chocolate in a heatproof bowl and set the bowl over a saucepan of simmering water, making sure the bowl doesn't touch the water. Stir the chocolate until melted. Remove the bowl from the heat and mix in the sugar and egg. Stir in the flour.

Transfer the mixture to a bowl and pour evenly among the paper liners. Bake for 20–25 minutes, or until cooked. Leave in the tin for 10 minutes, then transfer onto a wire rack to cool completely.

To make the ganache, place the chocolate and cream in a heatproof bowl. Set the bowl over a saucepan of simmering water, making sure the bowl doesn't touch the water. Once the chocolate has almost melted, remove the bowl from the heat and stir until the remaining chocolate has melted and the mixture is smooth. Allow to cool for about 8 minutes, or until thickened slightly.

Return the cakes to the cold tin to keep them stable while you spread 1 heaping teaspoon of ganache over each cake. Decorate with silver nonpareils.

MAKES 12

¼ cup plus 1 tablespoon unsalted butter
½ cup chopped milk chocolate
⅓ cup soft brown sugar
2 eggs, lightly beaten
½ cup self-rising flour, sifted

Ganache
½ cup chopped milk chocolate
2 tablespoons heavy cream
silver nonpareils, to decorate

Banana sour cream cupcakes

MAKES 24

¾ cup unsalted butter, softened
1 cup superfine sugar
3 eggs
2½ cups self-rising flour
½ teaspoon baking soda
¾ cup sour cream
2 tablespoons maple syrup
3 very ripe bananas, mashed

Honey cream frosting
scant ⅓ cup cream cheese, softened
2½ tablespoons unsalted butter, softened
1½ tablespoons honey
2 cups confectioners' sugar, sifted

Preheat the oven to 350°F. Line 24 standard muffin cups with paper liners.

Beat the butter and sugar in a large bowl using electric beaters for 5–6 minutes, or until light and fluffy. Add the eggs, one at a time, beating well after each addition.

Sift the flour and baking soda together. Add the sour cream and maple syrup to the mashed banana and mix well. Fold the flour mixture alternately with the banana mixture in the butter mixture until well combined.

Divide the mixture evenly among the paper liners. Bake for 15 minutes, or until a toothpick comes out clean when inserted into the center of a cake. Transfer onto a wire rack to cool.

To make the honey cream frosting, place the cream cheese and butter in a small bowl and beat with electric beaters until smooth. Add the honey and confectioners' sugar and beat until smooth and well combined. Decorate each cake generously with the frosting.

Marble cupcakes

MAKES 10

Preheat the oven to 350°F. Line 10 standard muffin cups with paper liners.

Beat the butter, sugar, and vanilla together with electric beaters until light and creamy. Add the eggs, one at a time, beating well after each addition. Sift the flours together and fold in alternately with the milk.

Divide the mixture into three equal portions. Add a few drops of pink food coloring to one portion and mix to combine. Add the cocoa to another portion and mix to combine. Divide the three colors evenly into each paper liner and gently swirl the mixture with a toothpick. Bake for 15 minutes, or until a toothpick comes out clean when inserted into the center of a cake. Transfer onto a wire rack to cool.

To make marble frosting, mix the confectioners' sugar, the butter, and enough hot water to make a spreadable frosting. Spread the frosting over each cake. Dip a toothpick in pink food coloring and swirl it through the frosting to create a marbled effect.

¾ cup unsalted butter, softened
¾ cup superfine sugar
1 teaspoon natural vanilla extract
3 eggs
1 cup self-rising flour
¼ cup all-purpose flour
½ cup milk
pink food coloring
2 tablespoons unsweetened cocoa
   powder, sifted

Marble frosting
2¼ cups confectioners' sugar, sifted
heaping ⅓ cup unsalted butter, softened
pink food coloring

41

Pecan and orange cupcakes

MAKES 16 or 24 mini

½ cup unsalted butter, softened
¾ cup superfine sugar
2 eggs
¾ cup ground pecans
3 teaspoons finely grated orange zest
1½ cups self-rising flour, sifted
½ cup milk

Cinnamon frosting
1 tablespoon unsalted butter, softened
¾ teaspoon ground cinnamon
1½ cups confectioners' sugar, sifted

Preheat the oven to 350°F. Line 16 standard (or 24 mini) muffin cups with paper liners.

Beat the butter and sugar with electric beaters until pale and creamy. Gradually add the eggs, one at a time, beating well after each addition. Add the ground pecans and orange zest, then use a metal spoon to gently fold in the flour alternately with the milk.

Divide the mixture evenly among the paper liners. Bake for 50–60 minutes (40 minutes for minis), or until a toothpick comes out clean when inserted into the center of a cake. Leave in the tin for 10 minutes, then transfer onto a wire rack to cool.

To make the cinnamon frosting, combine the butter, confectioners' sugar, and cinnamon in a small bowl with 1½ tablespoons of hot water. Set the bowl over a saucepan of simmering water, making sure the bowl doesn't touch the water, and stir until smooth and glossy. Remove from the heat. Decorate each cake with frosting.

White chocolate chip cupcakes

MAKES 12

Preheat the oven to 325°F. Line 12 standard muffin cups with paper liners.

Beat the butter and sugar in a large bowl with electric beaters until pale and creamy. Gradually add the eggs, one at a time, beating well after each addition. Add the vanilla extract and beat until combined. Fold in the flour alternately with the buttermilk, then fold in the chocolate chips.

Divide the mixture evenly among the paper liners until three-quarters full. Bake for 20 minutes, or until a toothpick comes out clean when inserted into the center of a cake. Leave the cakes in the tin for 5 minutes, then transfer onto a wire rack to cool.

½ cup unsalted butter, softened
¾ cup superfine sugar
2 eggs
1 teaspoon natural vanilla extract
2 cups self-rising flour, sifted
½ cup buttermilk
1¼ cups white chocolate chips

Rhubarb yogurt cupcakes

MAKES 24

1½ cups finely sliced fresh rhubarb, plus 24 extra pieces to garnish
2½ cups self-rising flour, sifted
1 cup superfine sugar
1 teaspoon natural vanilla extract
2 eggs, lightly beaten
½ cup plain yogurt
1 tablespoon rosewater
½ cup unsalted butter, melted

Preheat the oven to 350°F. Line 24 standard muffin cups with paper liners.

Combine the rhubarb, flour, and sugar in a bowl. Add the vanilla, egg, yogurt, rosewater, and the melted butter, stirring with a wooden spoon until the mixture is just combined.

Divide mixture evenly among the paper liners, then top with a piece of rhubarb. Bake for 15 minutes, or until a toothpick comes out clean when inserted into the center of a cake. Transfer onto a wire rack to cool.

Apple and raisin cupcakes

MAKES 12

Preheat the oven to 350°F. Line 12 standard muffin cups with paper liners.

Sift the flour into a large bowl and make a well in the center. Melt the butter and sugar in a small saucepan over a low heat, stirring until the sugar has dissolved. Remove from the heat. Combine the raisins and apple purée with the butter mixture. Pour into the well in the flour, along with the egg. Stir with a wooden spoon until combined.

Divide the mixture evenly among the paper liners. Bake for 15 minutes, or until a toothpick comes out clean when inserted into the center of a cake. Transfer onto a wire rack to cool completely.

To make the yogurt topping, combine the yogurt and sugar. Spread 1 tablespoon of topping over each cake.

1½ cups self-rising flour
scant ⅔ cup unsalted butter, chopped
¾ cup soft brown sugar
1 cup raisins, plus extra to garnish
½ cup apple purée
3 eggs, lightly beaten

Yogurt topping
1 cup plain yogurt
1 tablespoon soft brown sugar

Sweet afternoons

These elegant offerings call for an aromatic hot tea
to be sipped slowly from your finest china cup.

Pistachio and cardamom cupcakes

MAKES 24

1 cup unsalted pistachio pieces
½ teaspoon ground cardamom, plus extra
to sprinkle
scant ⅔ cup unsalted butter, chopped
1½ cups self-rising flour
¾ cup superfine sugar
3 eggs
½ cup plain yogurt

Lime syrup
½ cup superfine sugar
zest of 1 lime, white pith removed

Honey yogurt topping
1 cup plain yogurt
1 tablespoon honey

Preheat the oven to 350°F. Line 24 standard muffin cups with paper liners.

Place the pistachios and cardamom in a food processor and pulse until just chopped. Add the butter, flour, and superfine sugar, and pulse for 20 seconds, or until crumbly. Add the eggs and yogurt, and pulse until just combined.

Divide the mixture evenly among the paper liners. Bake for 15 minutes, or until a toothpick comes out clean when inserted into the center of a cake. Transfer onto a wire rack to cool.

To make the lime syrup, place the superfine sugar and 3½ fluid ounces of water in a small saucepan and stir over low heat until the sugar has dissolved. Bring to a boil, then add the zest and cook for 5 minutes. Strain. Brush the syrup over the cakes while they're still warm, then allow to cool.

To make the honey yogurt topping, place the yogurt and honey in a small bowl and stir until well combined. Decorate each cake with the honey yogurt and a sprinkle of ground cardamom.

Fruit tart cupcakes

MAKES 12

¾ cup unsalted butter, softened
¾ cup superfine sugar
1 teaspoon natural vanilla extract
3 eggs
1 cup self-rising flour
¼ cup all-purpose flour
½ cup milk
½ cup thick ready-made custard
1 kiwi fruit, peeled
1 cup strawberries
1 freestone peach, peeled
red grapes (about 4 to 6)
½ cup apricot jam

Preheat the oven to 350°F. Line 12 standard muffin cups with paper liners.

Beat the butter, sugar, and vanilla together with electric beaters until light and creamy. Add the eggs, one at a time, beating well after each addition. Sift the flours together and fold in alternately with the milk.

Divide the mixture evenly among the paper liners. Bake for 15 minutes, or until a toothpick comes out clean when inserted into the center of a cake. Transfer onto a wire rack to cool.

Cut the center out of each cake, leaving a ½-inch border. Fill each cavity with 2 teaspoons of custard. Cut the fruit and arrange over the custard. Heat the jam until runny. Lightly brush the jam over the top of each cake. Refrigerate until ready to serve.

Chocolate and almond cupcakes

MAKES 36

⅔ cup chopped bittersweet chocolate
½ cup ground almonds
¾ cup self-rising flour
4 eggs, separated
½ cup superfine sugar
2 tablespoons warm milk
chocolate flakes, to decorate
unsweetened cocoa powder, to sprinkle

Chocolate ganache
⅔ cup chopped bittersweet chocolate
heaping ⅓ cup unsalted butter

Preheat the oven to 350°F. Line 36 mini muffin cups with paper liners.

Place the chocolate in a food processor and process until finely ground. Add the ground almonds and flour, and process until just combined.

Beat the egg yolks and sugar with electric beaters for 2–3 minutes, or until thick and pale. Stir in the chocolate mixture, then the milk. Beat the egg whites in a clean bowl until soft peaks form. Gently fold the whites into the mixture with a metal spoon until just combined. Divide the mixture evenly among the paper liners. Bake for 10–12 minutes, or until a toothpick comes out clean when inserted into the center of a cake. Transfer onto a wire rack to cool.

To make the chocolate ganache, place the chocolate and butter in a small heatproof bowl over a saucepan of simmering water, making sure the bowl doesn't touch the water. Stir until smooth and combined. Refrigerate for 20 minutes, stirring occasionally until thickened.

Cut the center out of the cakes. Fill each cavity with 1 teaspoon of chocolate ganache, then decorate with chocolate flakes and cocoa.

Mandarin and chamomile cupcakes

MAKES 20

Preheat the oven to 350°F. Line 20 mini muffin cups with paper liners.

Place the milk and chamomile tea flowers into a saucepan and bring just to a boil. Stand for 5 minutes to infuse. Strain.

Place the butter, sugar, eggs, mandarin zest, and mandarin in a food processor, and process until almost smooth. Add the milk mixture, semolina, and flour, and process until smooth. Pour the mixture evenly among the paper liners. Bake for 8–10 minutes, or until a toothpick comes out clean when inserted into the center of a cake. Transfer onto a wire rack to cool.

To make the mandarin glaze, place the confectioners' sugar, zest, and enough juice to make a paste in a heatproof bowl. Set the bowl over a saucepan of simmering water, making sure the base of the bowl doesn't touch the water, and stir until runny. Remove from the heat but keep the bowl over the water. Spread the glaze over each cake and decorate with a chamomile flower.

¾ cup milk
¼ cup chamomile tea flowers, plus extra to decorate
scant ⅔ cup unsalted butter, chopped
1 cup superfine sugar
3 eggs
2 teaspoons finely grated mandarin zest
6 mandarins (about 10½ ounces), peeled, seeds removed
½ cup fine semolina
1¼ cups self-rising flour

Mandarin glaze
1¼ cups confectioners' sugar, sifted
1 teaspoon finely grated mandarin zest
2–3 tablespoons strained, fresh mandarin juice
chamomile tea flowers, to garnish

Individual blueberry cheesecakes

MAKES 6

Cheese mixture
½ cup superfine sugar
⅓ cup cream cheese

Blueberry sauce
1⅔ cups blueberries
1 tablespoon crème de cassis

1⅓ cups all-purpose flour
1 tablespoon baking powder
1 tablespoon unsalted butter, melted
1 teaspoon finely grated orange zest
1 egg
½ cup milk
18 blueberries, plus extra for filling
confectioners' sugar, to sprinkle

Preheat the oven to 350°F. Lightly grease 6 standard muffin cups with butter or oil.

To make the cheese mixture, put half the sugar in a bowl with the cream cheese and mix together well.

To make the blueberry sauce, put the blueberries in a blender or food processor with the liqueur and remaining sugar, and blend until smooth. Strain the mixture through a fine sieve to remove any blueberry seeds. Set the cheese mixture and sauce aside.

Sift the flour and baking powder together in a large bowl, and stir in the butter, orange zest, and ½ teaspoon of salt. In a separate bowl, beat the egg and milk together, then add to the dry ingredients and mix well until combined.

Divide half the mixture evenly among the cups. Add three of the extra blueberries and 1 teaspoon of cheese mixture in each cup, then top with the remaining batter mixture. Bake for 15 minutes, or until cooked and golden. Transfer onto a wire rack to cool slightly. To serve, put each cheesecake on a plate, drizzle with blueberry sauce, and sprinkle with confectioners' sugar.

Prune and ricotta cupcakes

MAKES 18

⅓ cup pitted prunes, chopped
1 tablespoon Marsala
1 cup ricotta cheese
½ cup superfine sugar
2 eggs
¼ cup whipping cream
¼ cup cornstarch, sifted
2 tablespoons self-rising flour, sifted
¼ cup grated bittersweet chocolate
confectioners' sugar, to sprinkle

Preheat the oven to 350°F. Line 18 mini muffin cups with paper liners.

Combine the prunes and Marsala in a small saucepan. Bring to a boil, then reduce the heat and simmer for 30 seconds, or until the Marsala is absorbed. Allow to cool.

Beat the ricotta and sugar with electric beaters for 2 minutes, or until light and creamy. Gradually add the eggs, one at a time, beating well after each addition. Add the cream and beat for 2 minutes. Using a metal spoon, fold in the sifted cornstarch and flour, the prune mixture, and the chocolate.

Divide the mixture evenly among the paper liners. Bake for 15–18 minutes, or until firm and lightly golden. Transfer onto a wire rack to cool. Sprinkle with confectioners' sugar just before serving.

Orange and lemon syrup cupcakes

MAKES 36

½ cup unsalted butter, chilled and chopped
1 cup superfine sugar
2 teaspoons finely grated lemon zest
2 teaspoons finely grated orange zest
3 eggs
½ cup milk
1½ cups self-rising flour, sifted

Lemon syrup
1 cup superfine sugar
zest of 1 lemon, thinly sliced
zest of 1 orange, thinly sliced

Preheat the oven to 350°F. Line 36 mini muffin cups with paper liners.

Place the butter, sugar, and lemon and orange zests in a saucepan, and stir over low heat until the sugar has dissolved. Transfer to a large bowl. Add the eggs, milk, and flour, and beat with electric beaters until just combined.

Divide the mixture evenly among the paper liners. Bake for 15 minutes, or until a toothpick comes out clean when inserted into the center of a cake. Transfer onto a wire rack to cool.

To make the lemon syrup, place 7 fluid ounces of water and the sugar in a saucepan over low heat, stirring until the sugar has dissolved. Add the lemon and orange zests, bring to a boil, and simmer for 10 minutes, stirring occasionally, or until lightly golden and syrupy.

Strain the syrup, reserving the zest. Decorate each cake with some strips of zest and pour over a little of the syrup.

Fluffy coconut cupcakes

MAKES 36

Preheat the oven to 350°F. Line 36 mini muffin cups with paper liners.

Combine the flour, coconut, and sugar in a bowl, and make a well in the center. Pour in the combined buttermilk, eggs, coconut extract, and butter into the well, and mix until combined.

Divide the mixture evenly among the paper liners. Bake for 12 minutes, or until a toothpick comes out clean when inserted into the center of a cake. Transfer onto a wire rack to cool.

To make the coconut frosting, combine the confectioners' sugar and coconut in a bowl. Add the butter, coconut extract, and enough hot water to make a spreadable frosting. Decorate each cake with a thick covering of frosting and sprinkle with toasted coconut.

2 cups self-rising flour, sifted
½ cup unsweetened dried coconut
1 cup superfine sugar
1 cup buttermilk
2 eggs, lightly beaten
1 teaspoon natural coconut extract
½ cup unsalted butter, melted

Coconut frosting
2¼ cups confectioners' sugar
1½ cups unsweetened dried coconut
¼ cup plus 1 tablespoon unsalted butter, softened
½ teaspoon natural coconut extract
2 tablespoons hot water
unsweetened dried coconut, lightly toasted, to sprinkle

Hazelnut cream sponge cakes

MAKES 16

4 eggs, separated
½ cup superfine sugar
½ cup self-rising flour
⅔ cup ground hazelnuts
1 tablespoon unsalted butter

Hazelnut frosting
½ cup chocolate hazelnut spread
heaping ½ cup unsalted butter, softened
½ cup confectioners' sugar, sifted

Preheat the oven to 350°F. Grease a shallow 8-inch square cake tin and line the base with parchment paper.

Beat the egg whites in a clean bowl with electric beaters until soft peaks form. Gradually add the sugar, beating until thick and glossy. Beat the egg yolks into the mixture, one at a time.

Sift the flour over the mixture, add the ground hazelnuts, and fold in with a metal spoon. Melt the butter with 2 tablespoons of boiling water in a small bowl, then fold into the sponge mixture. Pour the mixture into the tin and bake for 25 minutes, or until a toothpick comes out clean when inserted into the center of the cake. Leave in the tin for 5 minutes before turning out onto a wire rack to cool. Cut the sponge in half horizontally through the center.

To make the hazelnut frosting, beat the chocolate hazelnut spread and butter with electric beaters until very creamy. Beat in the confectioners' sugar, then gradually add 3 teaspoons of boiling water, and beat until smooth. Spread the frosting over the base of the sponge, then replace the top layer. Refrigerate until the filling is firm, then cut into squares, and place inside paper liners.

Streusel cupcakes

MAKES 24

Preheat the oven to 350°F. Line 24 standard muffin cups with paper liners.

To make the custard, place the egg yolks, sugar, and custard powder in a bowl, and whisk until pale. Heat the milk in a small saucepan until almost boiling. Remove from the heat, then gradually whisk into the egg mixture. Return the combined mixture to the cleaned saucepan and stir constantly over low heat until the mixture boils and thickens. Refrigerate until cold.

To make the topping, mix all the ingredients together in a bowl, until the mixture resembles coarse breadcrumbs.

Beat the butter, sugar, and vanilla together with electric beaters until light and creamy. Add the eggs, one at a time, beating well after each addition. Sift the flours and pumpkin pie spice together and fold in alternately with the golden raisins and milk. Swirl the custard through the mixture, but do not overmix. Divide the mixture evenly among the paper liners. Sprinkle the topping over the cakes. Bake for 14–15 minutes, or until a toothpick comes out clean when inserted into the center of a cake. Transfer onto a wire rack to cool.

Custard
3 egg yolks
2 tablespoons superfine sugar
2 tablespoons instant custard powder
1 cup milk
1 teaspoon natural vanilla extract

Topping
½ cup all-purpose flour
⅔ cup finely chopped walnuts
½ cup soft brown sugar
scant ⅓ cup unsalted butter, melted
1 teaspoon ground cinnamon

¾ cup unsalted butter, softened
¾ cup superfine sugar
1 teaspoon natural vanilla extract
3 eggs
1 cup self-rising flour
¼ cup all-purpose flour
1 teaspoon pumpkin pie spice
½ cup golden raisins
½ cup milk

Passionfruit cupcakes

¾ cup unsalted butter, softened
¾ cup superfine sugar
1 teaspoon natural vanilla extract
3 eggs
½ cup cream cheese, softened
1 tablespoon fresh passionfruit pulp
(about 1 passionfruit)
1 cup self-rising flour
¼ cup all-purpose flour
¼ cup milk

Passionfruit frosting
1¼ cups whipping cream
1½ tablespoons confectioners' sugar, sifted
2 tablespoons fresh passionfruit pulp
(about 2 passionfruit)

Preheat the oven to 350°F. Line 15 standard muffin cups with paper liners.

Beat the butter, sugar, and vanilla together with electric beaters until light and creamy. Add the eggs, one at a time, beating well after each addition. Add the cream cheese and passionfruit, and beat until smooth. Sift the flours together and fold in alternately with the milk.

Divide the mixture evenly among the paper liners. Bake for 15 minutes, or until a toothpick comes out clean when inserted into the center of a cake. Transfer onto a wire rack to cool.

To make the passionfruit frosting, beat the cream and confectioners' sugar together until soft peaks form. Cut the center out of each cake leaving a ½-inch border. Spoon the cream into a piping bag fitted with a ½-inch star nozzle. Decorate each cake with piped cream and top with the passionfruit.

Baklava cupcakes

MAKES 36

Filling
½ cup walnuts, chopped
⅓ cup blanched almonds, chopped
½ cup raw sugar
2 teaspoons ground cinnamon
2½ tablespoons unsalted butter, melted

¾ cup unsalted butter, softened
¾ cup soft brown sugar
3 eggs
1 cup self-rising flour
¼ cup all-purpose flour
½ cup buttermilk
¼ cup honey, warmed

Preheat the oven to 350°F. Line 36 mini muffin cups with paper liners.

Combine the filling ingredients in a bowl and set aside.

Beat the butter and sugar in a bowl with electric beaters until light and creamy. Add the eggs, one at a time, beating well after each addition. Fold in the sifted flours alternately with the milk, and stir until smooth and combined.

Divide half the mixture evenly among the paper liners. Sprinkle half the filling over the mixture, then spoon the remaining mixture over the top. Sprinkle over the remaining filling. Bake for 10–12 minutes, or until a toothpick comes out clean when inserted into the center of a cake. Brush warm honey over the cakes while they are still hot.

Plum and almond cupcakes

MAKES 18

1½ cups self-rising flour
1½ teaspoons ground cinnamon
heaping ⅓ cup unsalted butter, melted
1 cup soft brown sugar
3 eggs, lightly beaten
⅓ cup blanched almonds, finely chopped
1 pound 13-ounce can pitted plums
in natural juice, drained and chopped
dried rose petals, to decorate

White chocolate cream frosting
1⅓ cups chopped white chocolate
½ cup whipping cream
heaping ¾ cup cream cheese, softened
⅓ cup confectioners' sugar, sifted
red food coloring

Preheat the oven to 325°F. Line 18 standard muffin cups with paper liners.

Sift the flour and cinnamon together in a bowl. Add the butter, sugar, eggs, almonds, and plums, and mix with electric beaters until combined.

Divide the mixture evenly among the paper liners. Bake for 15 minutes, or until a toothpick comes out clean when inserted into the center of a cake. Transfer onto a wire rack to cool.

To make the white chocolate cream frosting, combine the chocolate and cream in a small saucepan and stir over low heat until the chocolate has melted. Place the chocolate mixture, cream cheese, and confectioners' sugar in a bowl, and beat with electric beaters until smooth. Add a few drops of red food coloring and blend evenly. Cover the bowl and refrigerate for 2 minutes, or until slightly firm. Beat the mixture again for a few seconds until smooth.

Spread the frosting over each cake and decorate with the dried rose petals.

Mango cakes with lime syrup

MAKES 8

Preheat the oven to 400°F. Grease 8 large muffin cups, then line with the mango slices.

Beat the butter and sugar in a bowl with electric beaters until light and creamy. Gradually add the eggs, one at a time, beating well after each addition. Fold in the flour, then add the almonds and coconut milk.

Divide the mixture evenly among the cups. Bake for 25 minutes, or until a toothpick comes out clean when inserted into the center of a cake.

To make the lime syrup, place the lime juice, sugar, and ½ cup of water in a small saucepan and stir over low heat until the sugar dissolves. Increase the heat and simmer for 10 minutes.

Pierce holes in each cake with a toothpick. Drizzle the syrup over the top and leave for 5 minutes to soak up the liquid. Turn out onto plates and serve.

1 pound 14-ounce can mango slices in syrup, drained
¾ cup unsalted butter, softened
1 cup superfine sugar
4 eggs
1 cup self-rising flour
⅓ cup ground almonds
⅓ cup coconut milk

Lime syrup
⅓ cup lime juice
½ cup superfine sugar

Madeira cupcakes

MAKES 12

¾ cup unsalted butter, softened
¾ cup superfine sugar
3 eggs
1⅓ cups all-purpose flour
2 teaspoons baking powder
1 teaspoon finely grated orange zest
1 tablespoon orange juice

Orange frosting
2 cups confectioners' sugar, sifted, plus extra
to sprinkle
½ cup unsalted butter, softened
1 tablespoon orange juice

Preheat the oven to 350°F. Line 12 standard muffin cups with paper liners.

Beat the butter and sugar in a bowl with electric beaters until pale and light. Add the eggs, one at a time, beating well after each addition. Sift the flour and baking powder together. Fold the flour, orange zest, and juice into the butter mixture until combined.

Divide the mixture evenly among the paper liners. Bake for 12–15 minutes, or until a toothpick comes out clean when inserted into the center of a cake. Transfer onto a wire rack to cool completely.

To make the orange frosting, place the confectioners' sugar, butter, and juice in a large bowl, and beat with electric beaters until smooth and well combined. Decorate each cake with frosting and sprinkle with confectioners' sugar.

Chestnut cupcakes

MAKES 36

½ cup unsalted butter, softened
1 cup superfine sugar
1 teaspoon natural vanilla extract
½ cup unsweetened chestnut purée
3 eggs
⅓ cup milk
1¼ cups self-rising flour, sifted
1 teaspoon baking powder
36 frosting flower decorations

Chocolate glaze
1⅔ cups chopped bittersweet chocolate
¾ cup whipping cream

Preheat the oven to 350°F. Line 36 mini muffin cups with paper liners.

Beat the butter, sugar, and vanilla with electric beaters until light and creamy. Add the chestnut purée and beat for 1 minute, or until just combined. Add the eggs, one at a time, beating well after each addition. Fold in the milk, flour, and baking powder, and stir with a wooden spoon until the ingredients are just combined.

Divide the mixture evenly among the paper liners. Bake for 15 minutes, or until a toothpick comes out clean when inserted into the center of a cake. Transfer onto a wire rack to cool completely.

To make the chocolate glaze, combine the chocolate and cream in a small saucepan. Stir over low heat until the chocolate has melted and the mixture is smooth. Remove from the heat and cool slightly.

Dip the top of each cake into the glaze to coat and decorate each with a frosting flower.

Saffron spice cupcakes

MAKES 24

¾ cup orange juice
3 teaspoons finely grated orange zest
¼ teaspoon saffron threads
2 eggs
1 cup confectioners' sugar
1 teaspoon natural vanilla extract
1½ cups self-rising flour
1½ cups ground almonds
heaping ⅓ cup unsalted butter, melted

Candied saffron threads
½ teaspoon saffron threads
2 tablespoons orange juice

Mascarpone cream
1 cup plus 2 tablespoons mascarpone cheese
½ cup confectioners' sugar, sifted
¼ teaspoon ground cardamom

Preheat the oven to 350°F. Line 24 standard muffin cups with paper liners.

Combine the orange juice, zest, and saffron in a small saucepan, and bring to a boil. Reduce the heat and simmer for 1 minute. Leave to cool.

Beat the eggs, confectioners' sugar, and vanilla with electric beaters until light and creamy. Fold in the sifted flour, almonds, orange juice mixture, and butter with a metal spoon until combined. Divide the mixture evenly among the paper liners. Bake for 18–20 minutes, or until a toothpick comes out clean when inserted into the center of a cake. Transfer onto a wire rack to cool.

To make the candied saffron threads, place the saffron and orange juice in a small saucepan and bring to a simmer for 1 minute. Strain and discard the orange juice. Set the saffron threads aside.

To make the mascarpone cream, place the mascarpone, sugar, and cardamom in a small bowl, and mix to combine (be careful not to overmix or it may curdle). Decorate each cake with piped cream and top with the saffron threads.

Coconut, ginger, and lime cupcakes

MAKES 36

Preheat the oven to 350°F. Line 36 mini muffin cups with paper liners.

Beat the butter, sugar, and lime zest with electric beaters until light and creamy. Add the eggs, one at a time, beating well after each addition. Add the ginger. Stir in the sifted flour and the coconut alternately with the milk.

Divide the mixture evenly among the paper liners. Bake for 15 minutes, or until a toothpick comes out clean when inserted into the center of a cake. Transfer onto a wire rack to cool.

To make the lime frosting, combine all of the ingredients, adding enough lime juice to make a smooth, runny frosting. Decorate each cake with frosting.

scant ⅔ cup unsalted butter, softened
¾ cup superfine sugar
2 teaspoons finely grated lime zest
2 eggs
¼ cup finely chopped candied ginger
1¾ cups self-rising flour
½ cup unsweetened dried coconut
¾ cup milk

Lime frosting
1 cup confectioners' sugar, sifted
2 teaspoons unsalted butter, softened
1 teaspoon finely grated lime zest
2 tablespoons lime juice

Index

Thunder Bay Press

An imprint of the Baker & Taylor Publishing Group
10350 Barnes Canyon Road, San Diego, CA 92121
www.thunderbaybooks.com

ISBN-13: 978-1-60710-226-7
ISBN-10: 1-60710-226-9

Printed in China.

1 2 3 4 5 15 14 13 12 11

OVEN GUIDE: You may find cooking times vary depending on the oven you are using.
For fan-forced ovens, as a general rule, set the oven temperature to 25°F lower than indicated in the recipe.